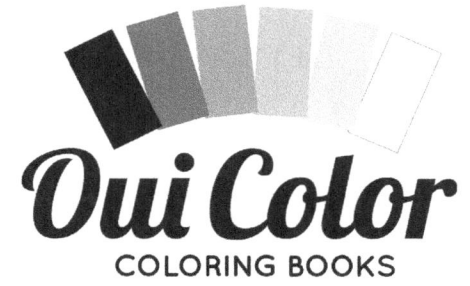

Oui Color
COLORING BOOKS

Fall Harvest

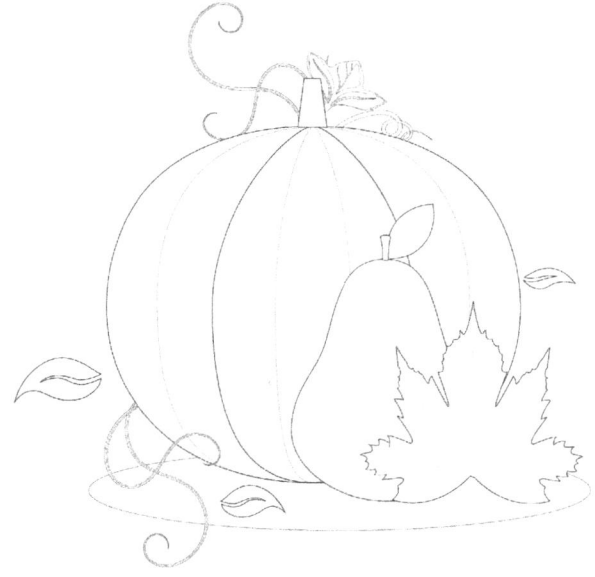

20 Fall Harvest Themed Images to Color

By Sandra Jean-Pierre

ISBN-13: 9781724141378

DEDICATION

Thank You Tracey Chaykin for encouraging me, being my sounding board
and filling my world with color <3
I'd also like to thank my sister E, for still not ever coloring within the lines.
The Nephew for loving my designs,
Penelope Dog for her unconditional love and the Universe, for grace, inspiration and gifts.
Thanks also goes out to the entire Oui Color Facebook Group for inspiring me daily! <3

ABOUT THE AUTHOR

Sandra Jean-Pierre is an author, poet, graphic designer, amateur photographer
and mean crafter of crocheted afghans.

Follow her on Twitter: @sandrajp

Follow *Oui Color* on
Twitter: @OuiColor
IG: OuiColor
Pinterest: www.pinterest.com/ouicolor
NEW! Facebook Coloring Group - Join Us:
www.OuiColor.com/FacebookGroup

You can now upload your completed #OuiCeations
to the OuiGallery:
www.ouicolor.com/OuiGallery

FREE COLORING PAGES!
Visit www.ouicolor.com/FreeColoringPages
for more info.

#InspireYourCreativity

Oui Color
COLORING BOOKS

Fall Harvest

Below are examples of the patterns you will find in this book.

Blotter Sheets are placed in the back of this book for your convenience.

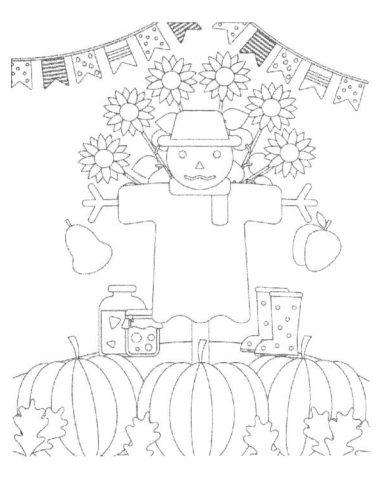

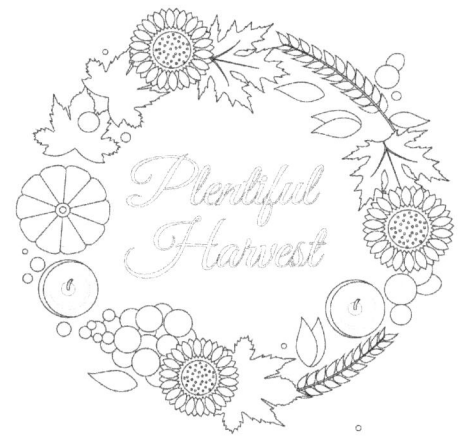

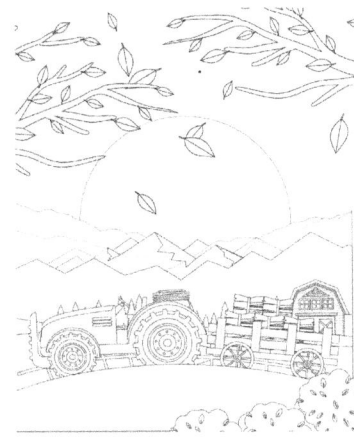

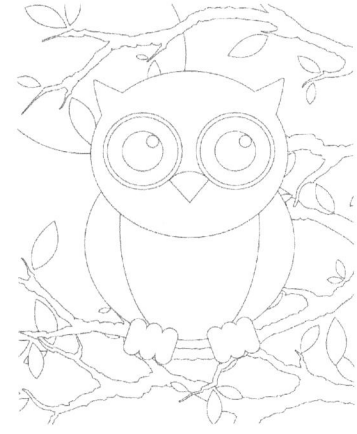

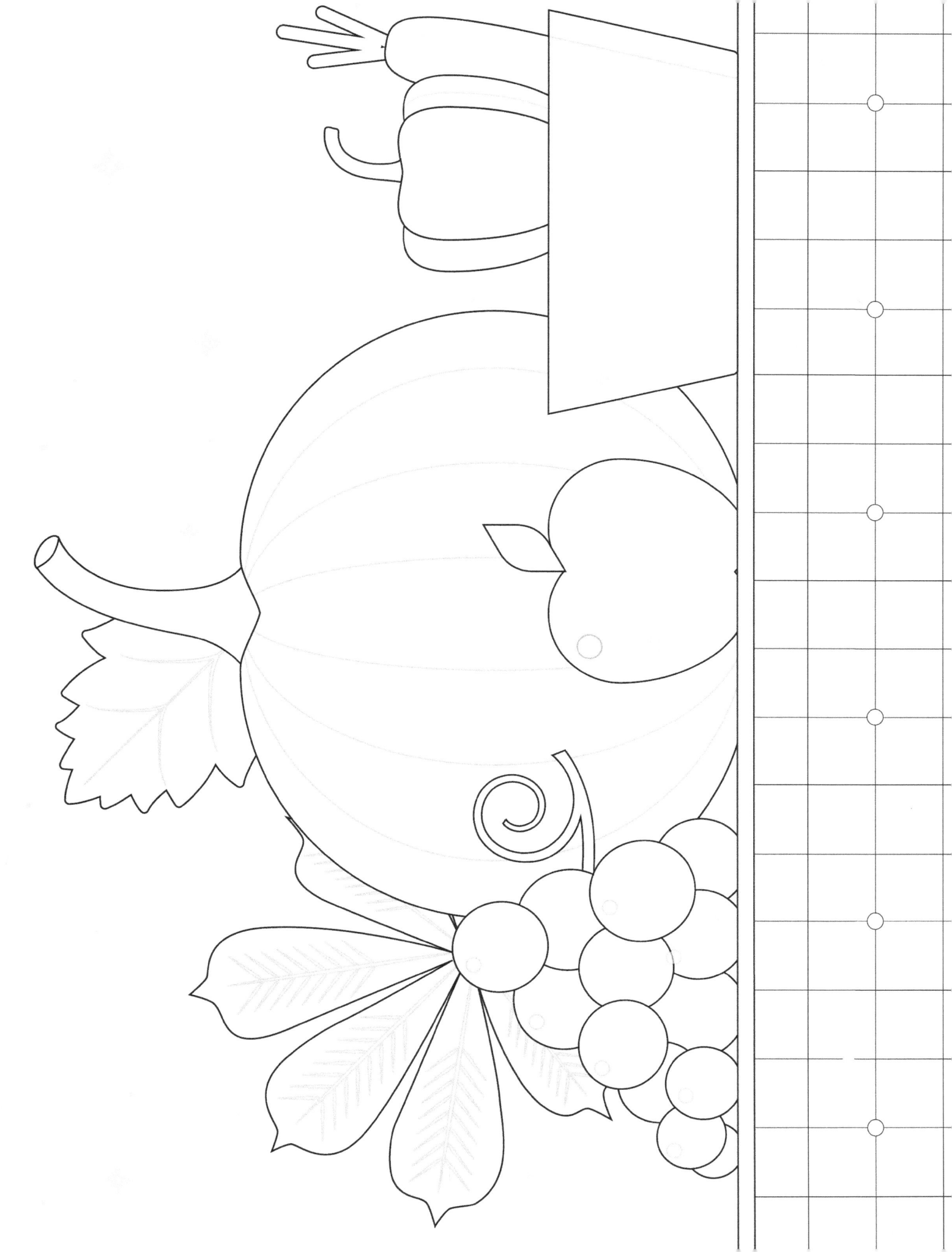

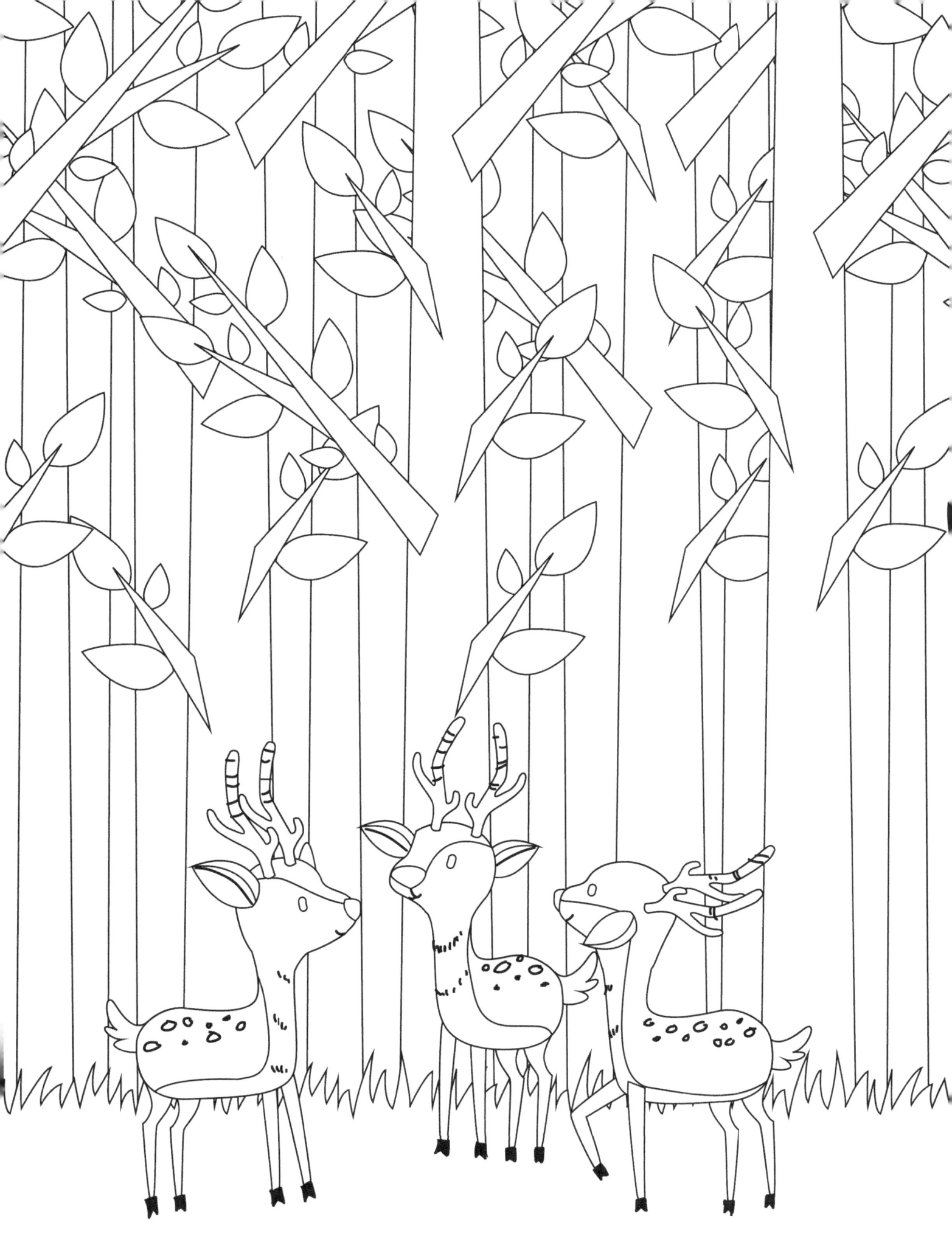

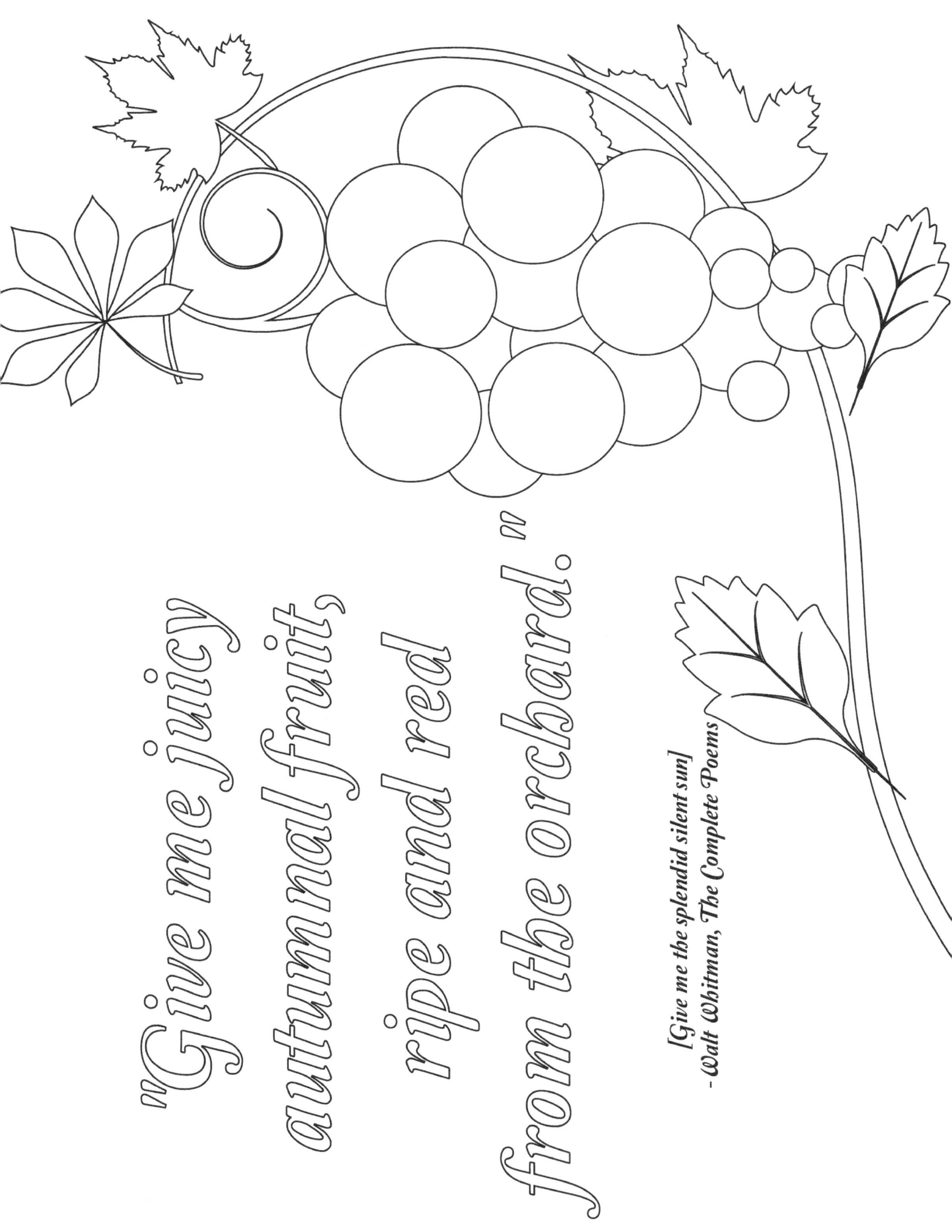

"Give me juicy autumnal fruit, ripe and red from the orchard."

[Give me the splendid silent sun]
- Walt Whitman, The Complete Poems

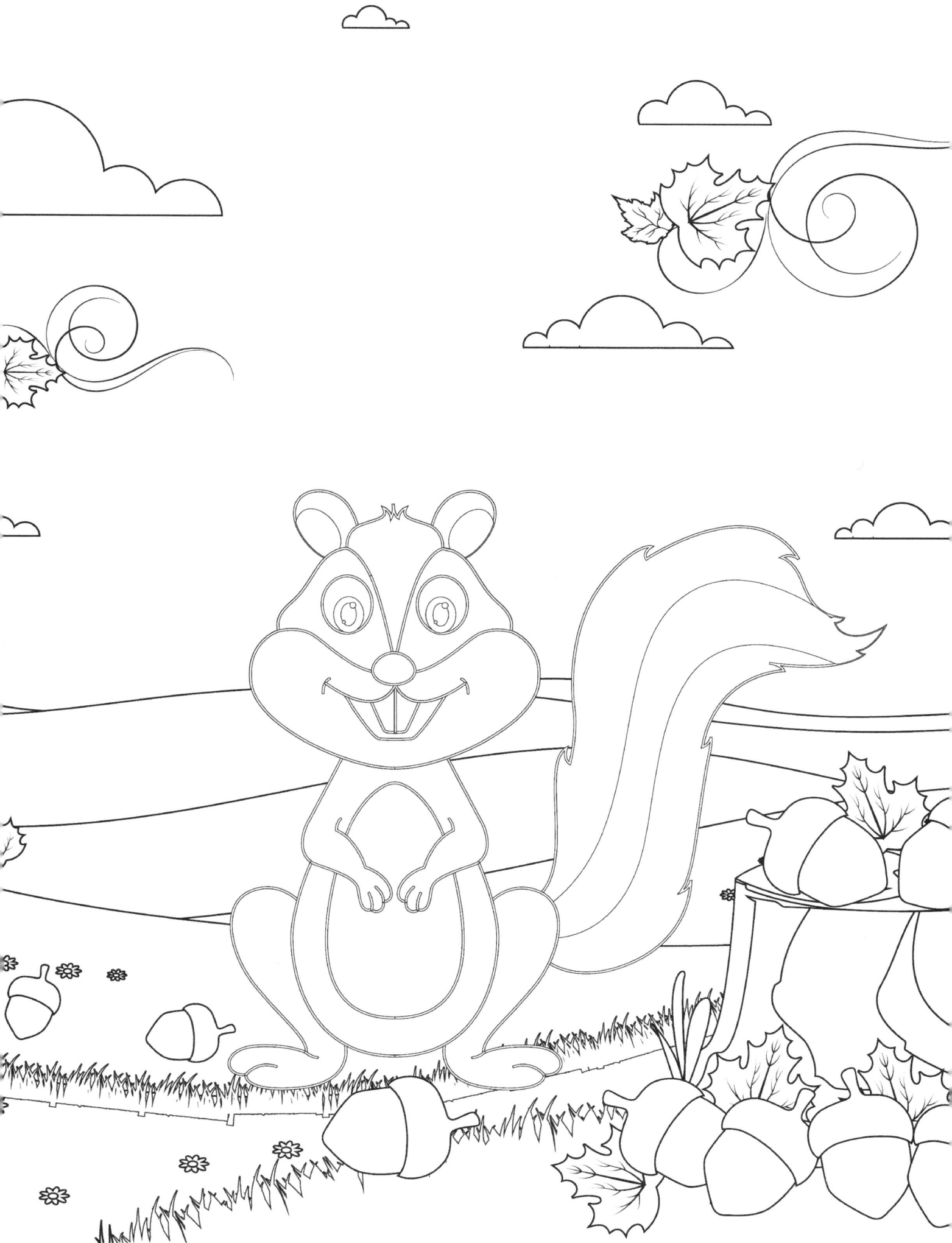

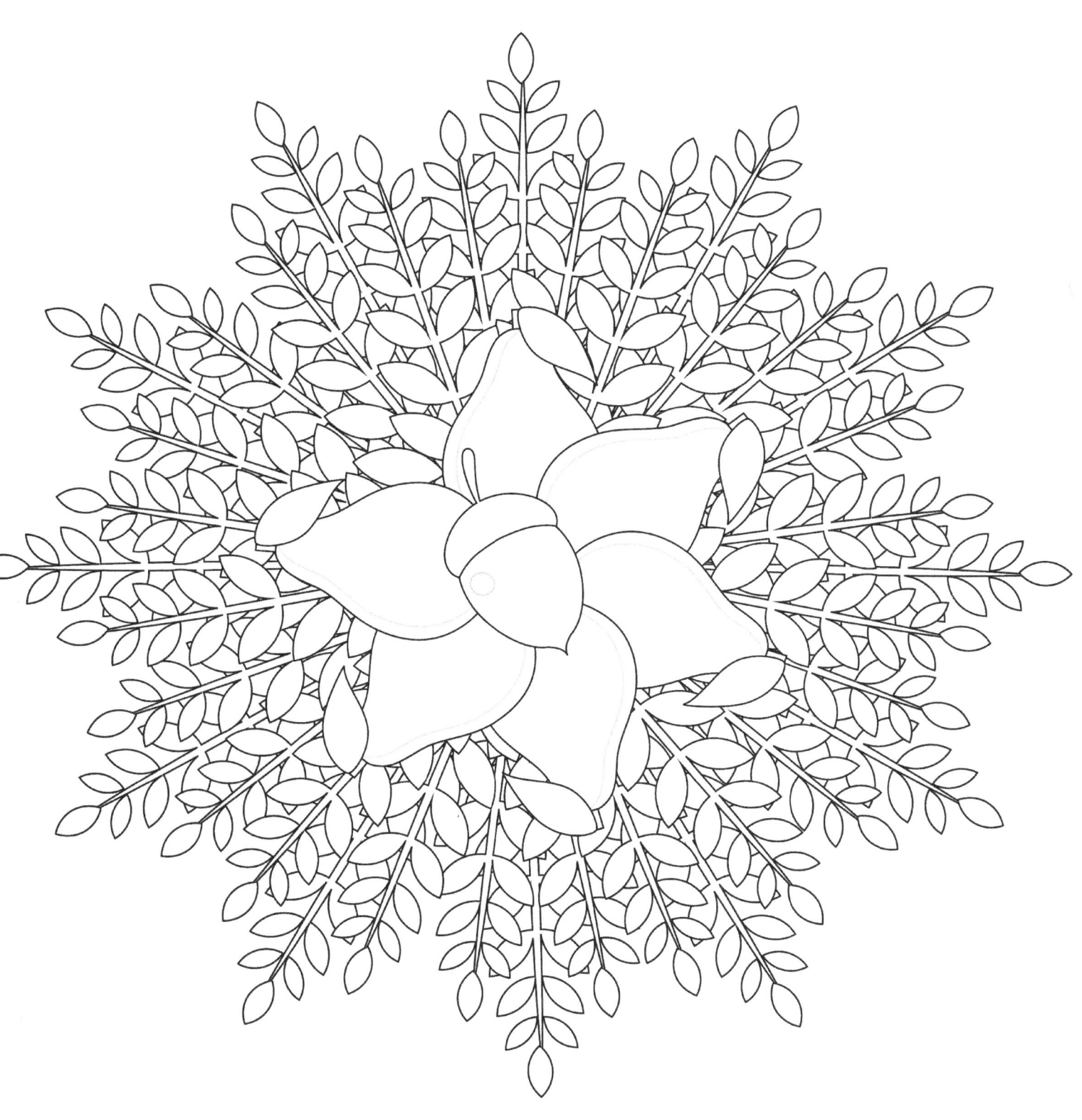

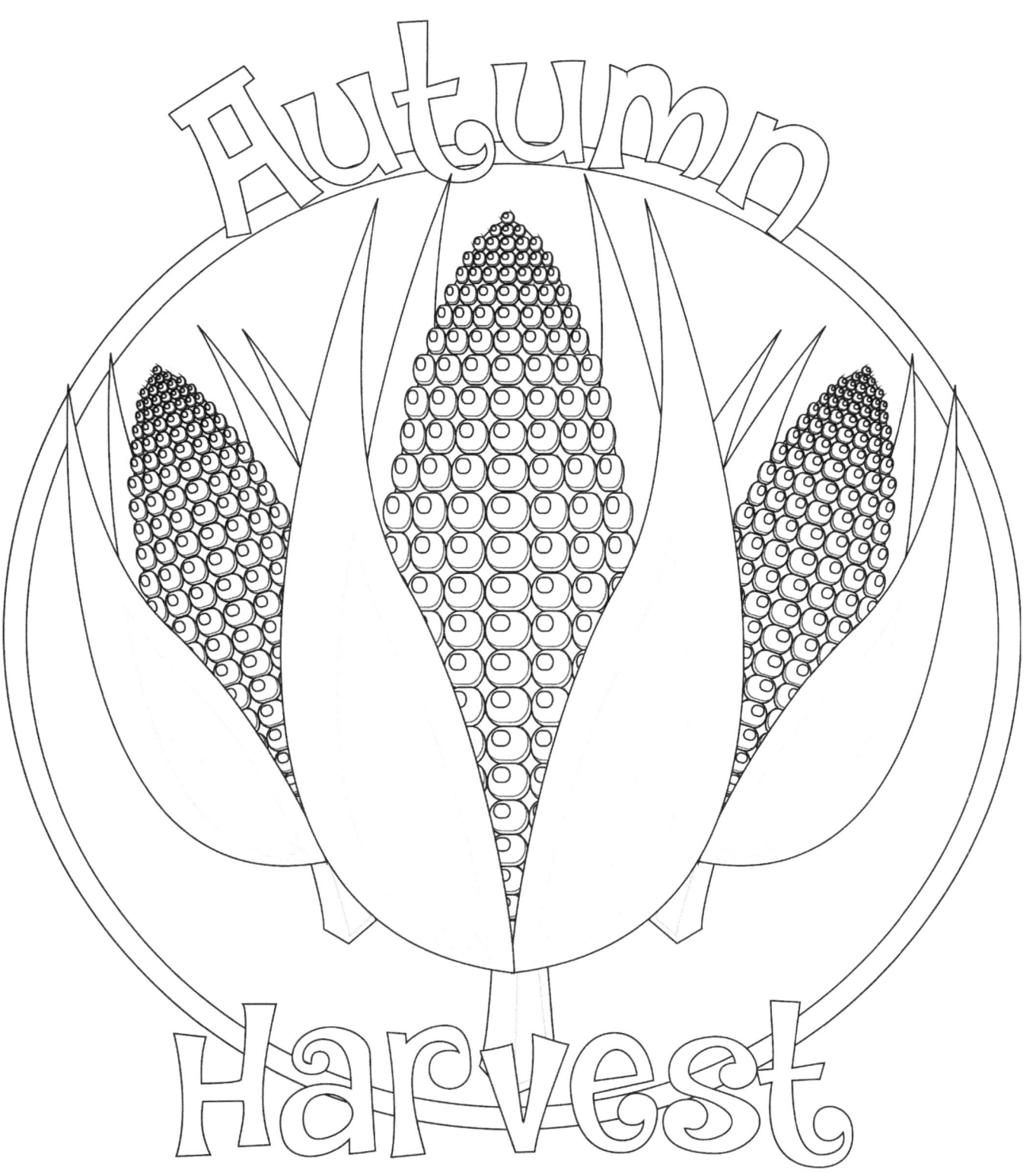

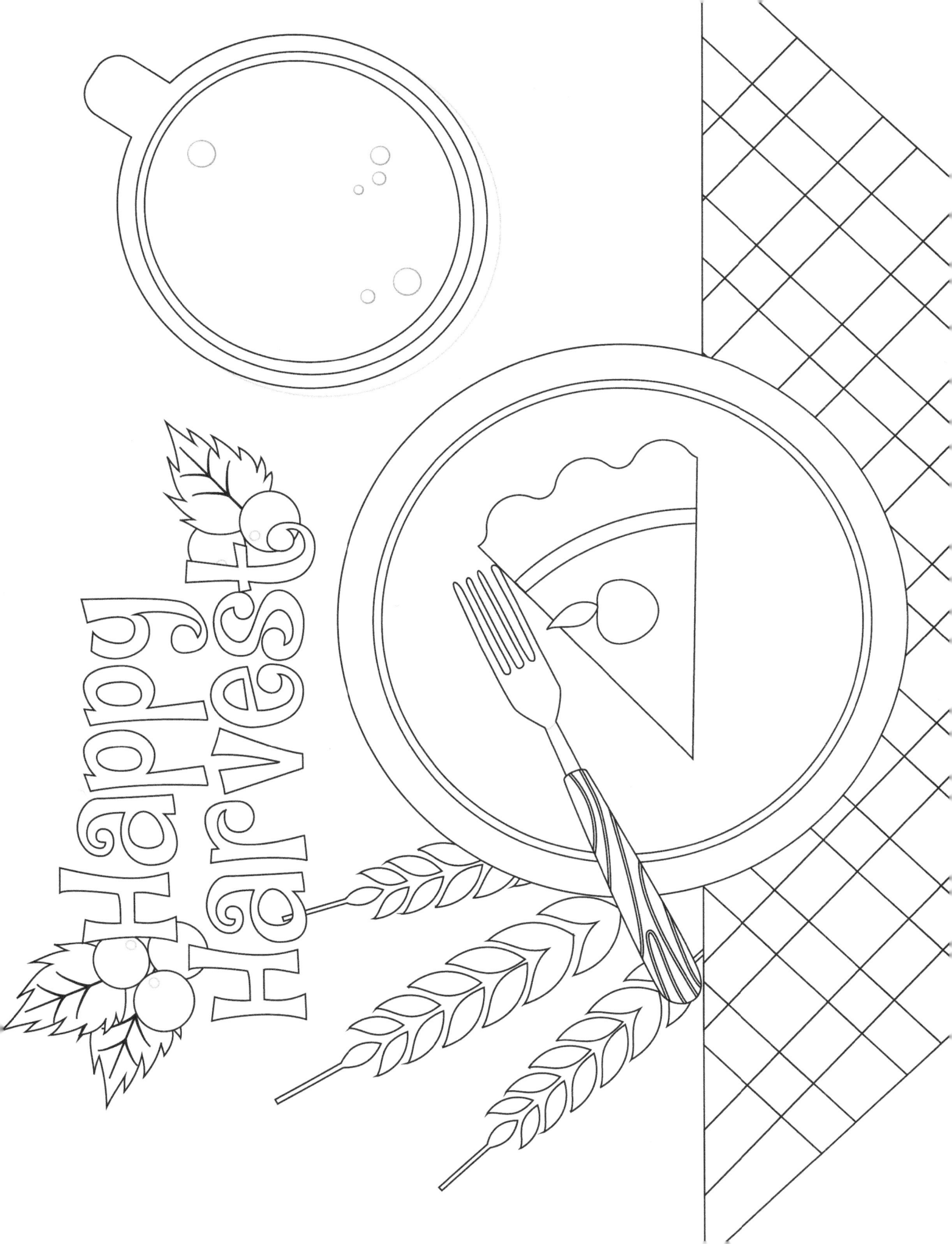

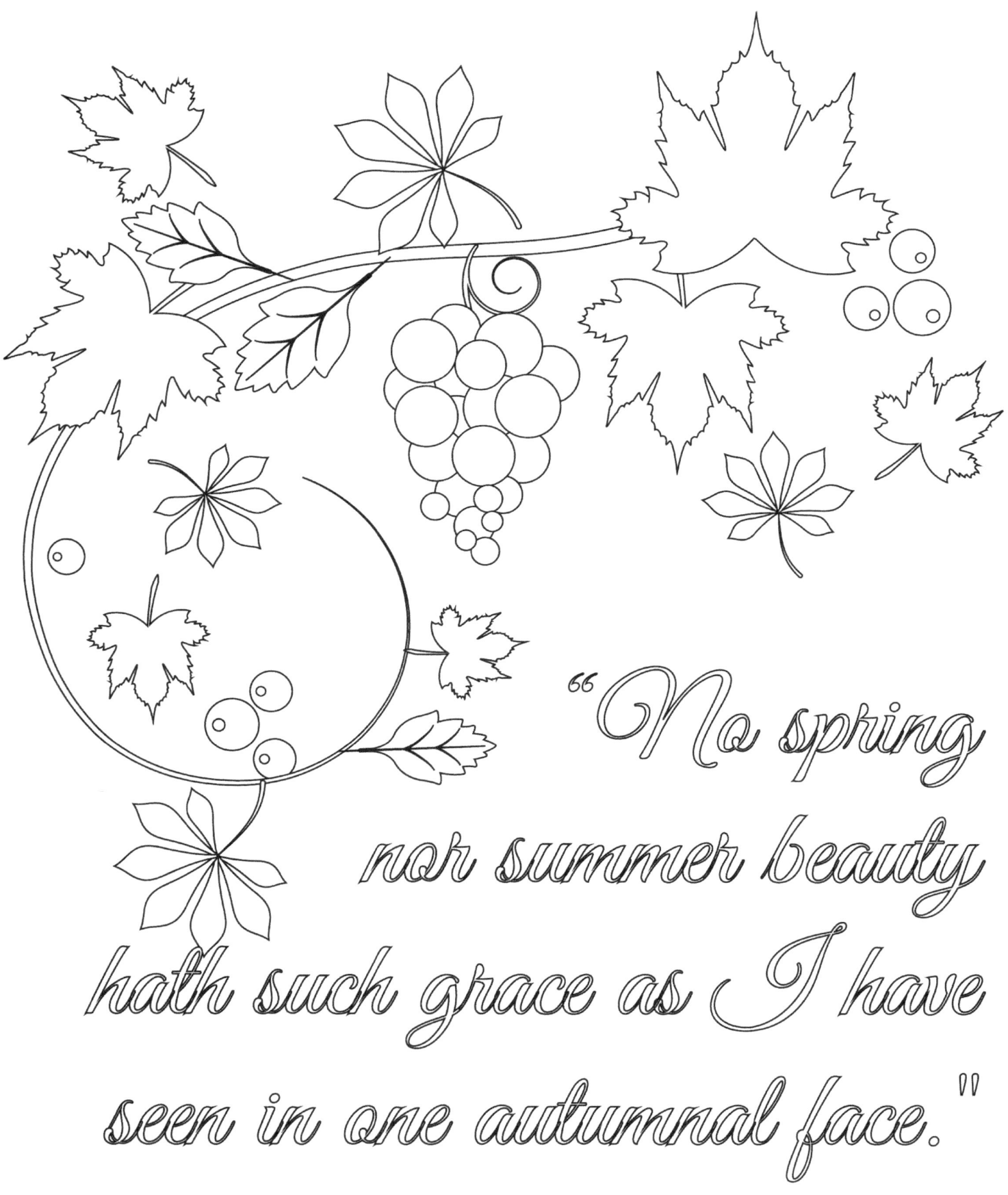

"No spring nor summer beauty hath such grace as I have seen in one autumnal face."

[The Autumnal]
–John Donne, The Complete Poetry and Selected Prose

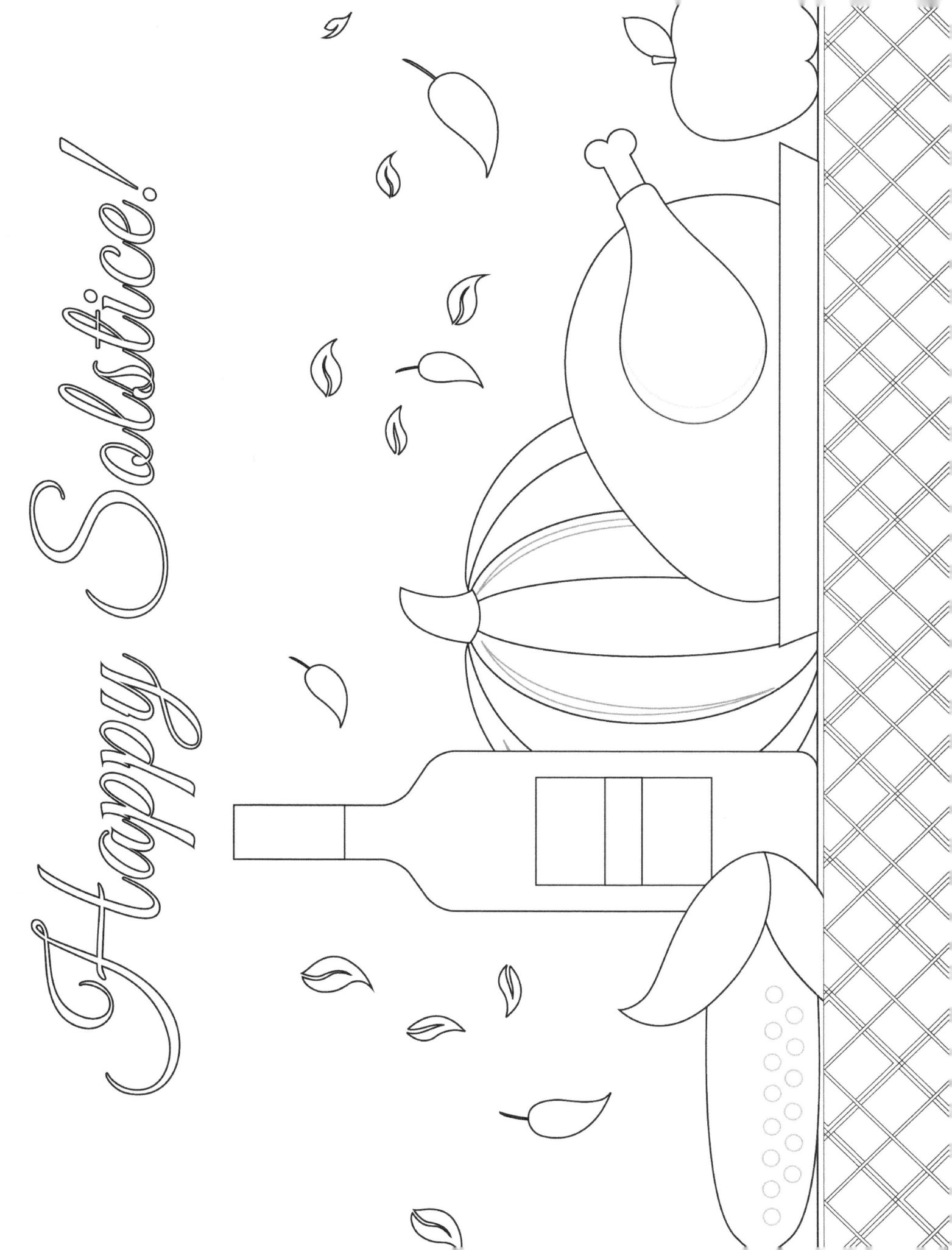

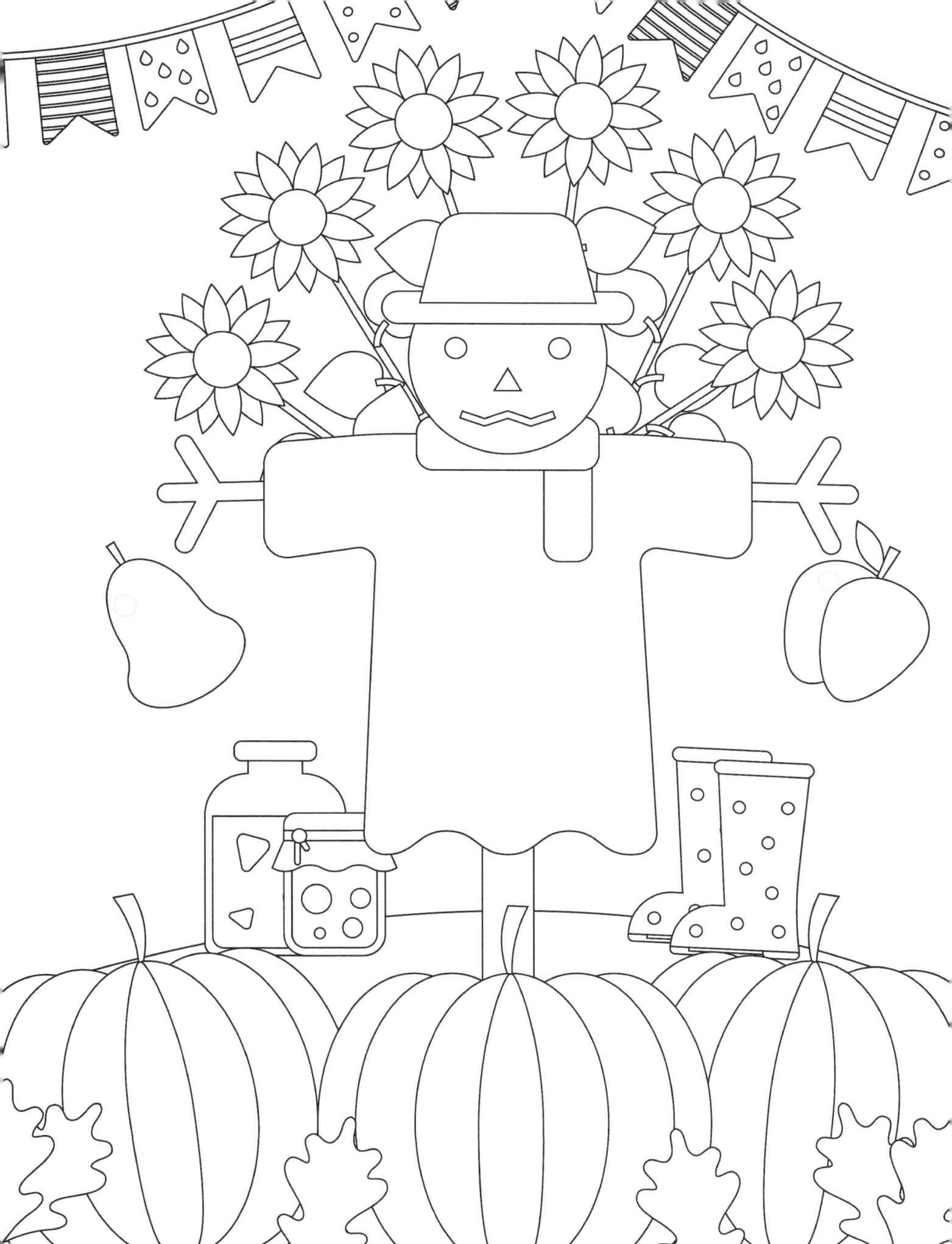

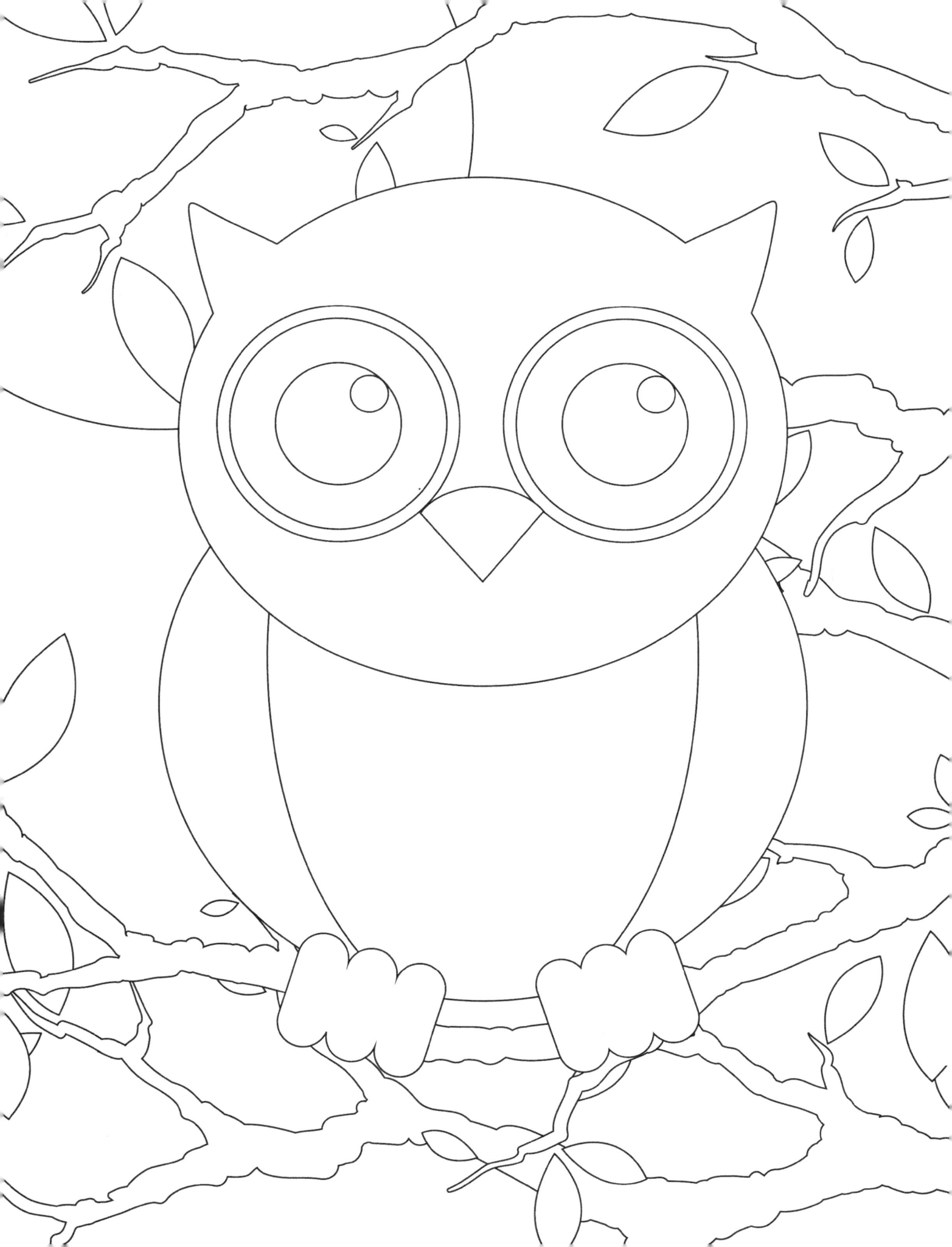

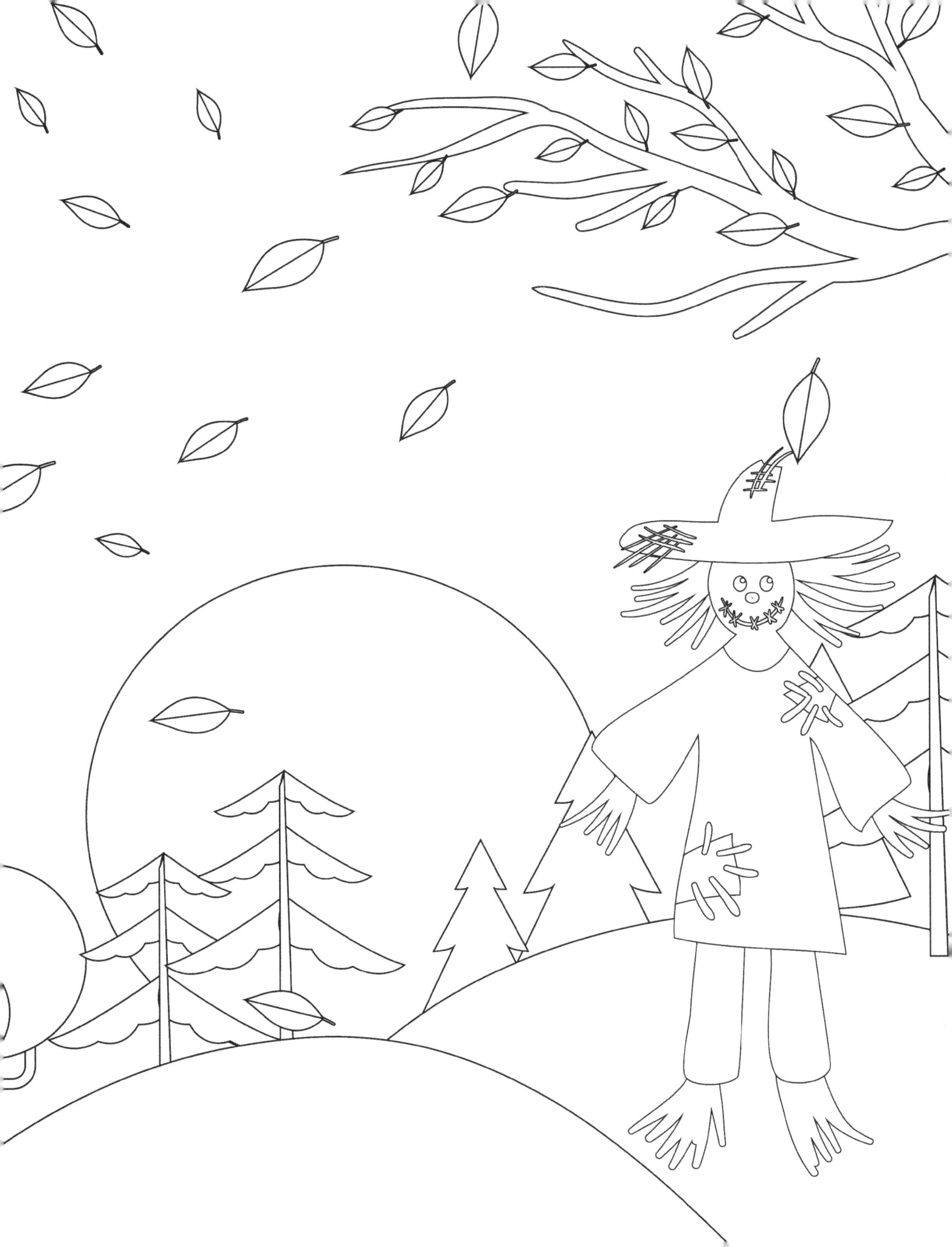

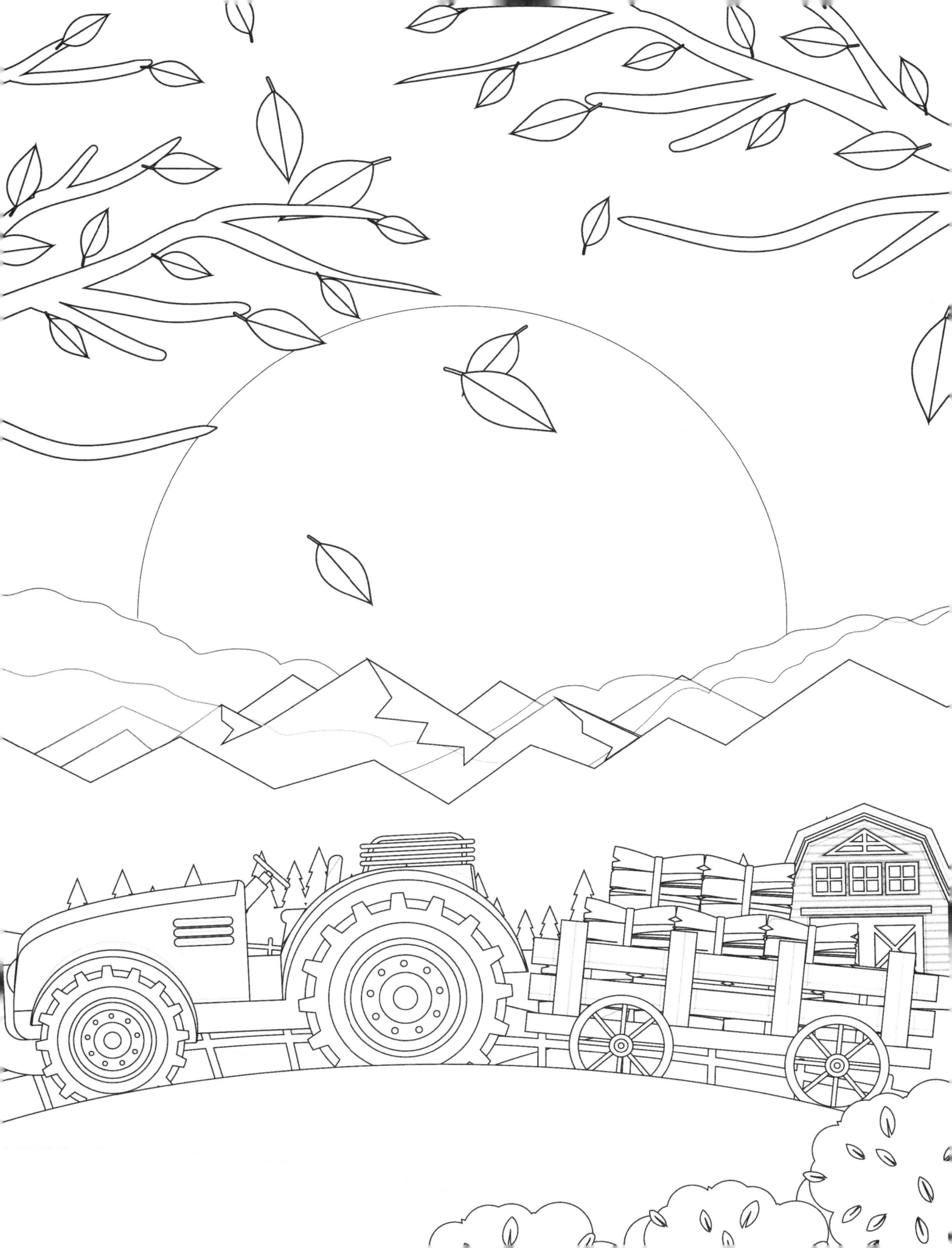

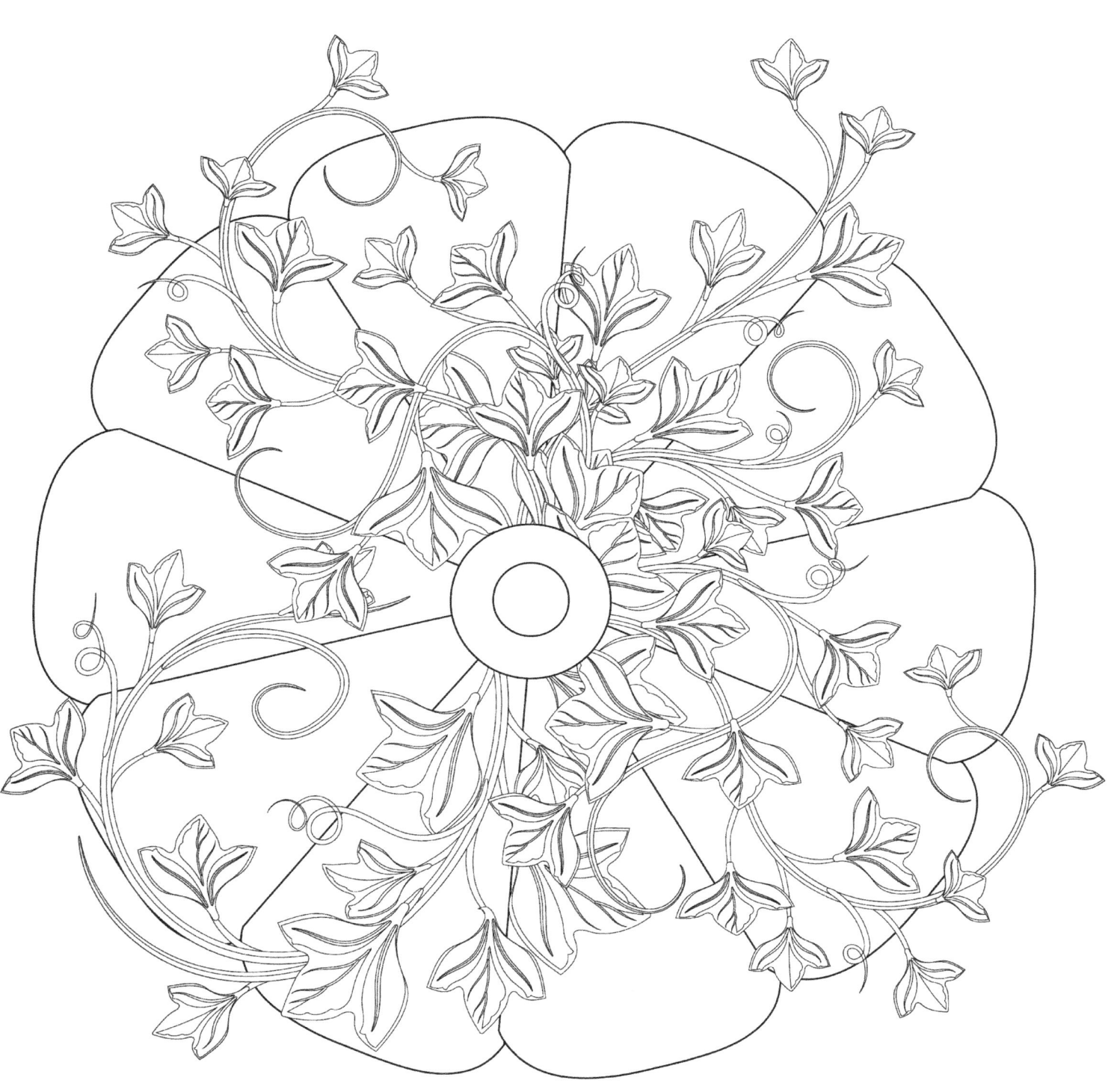

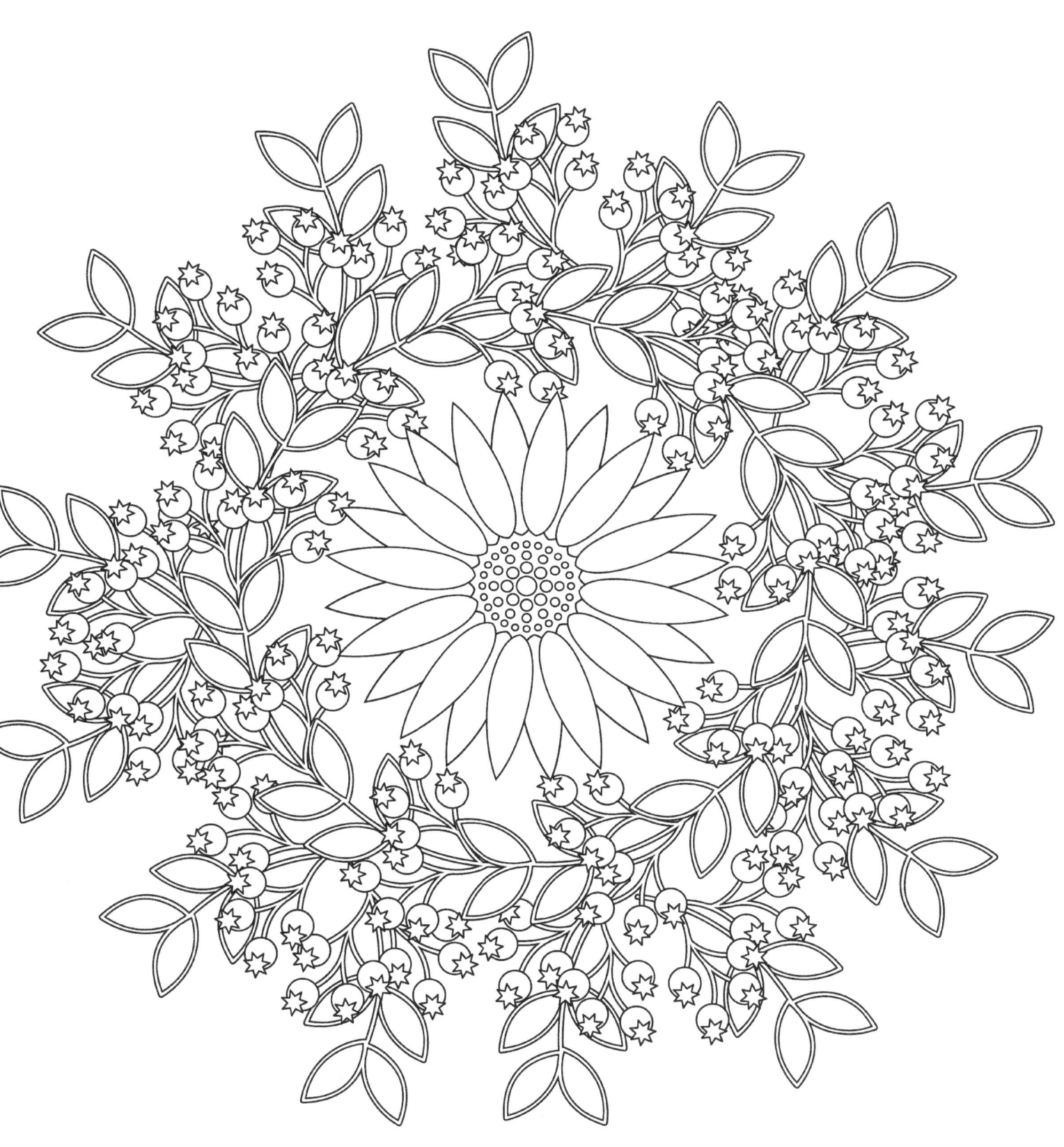

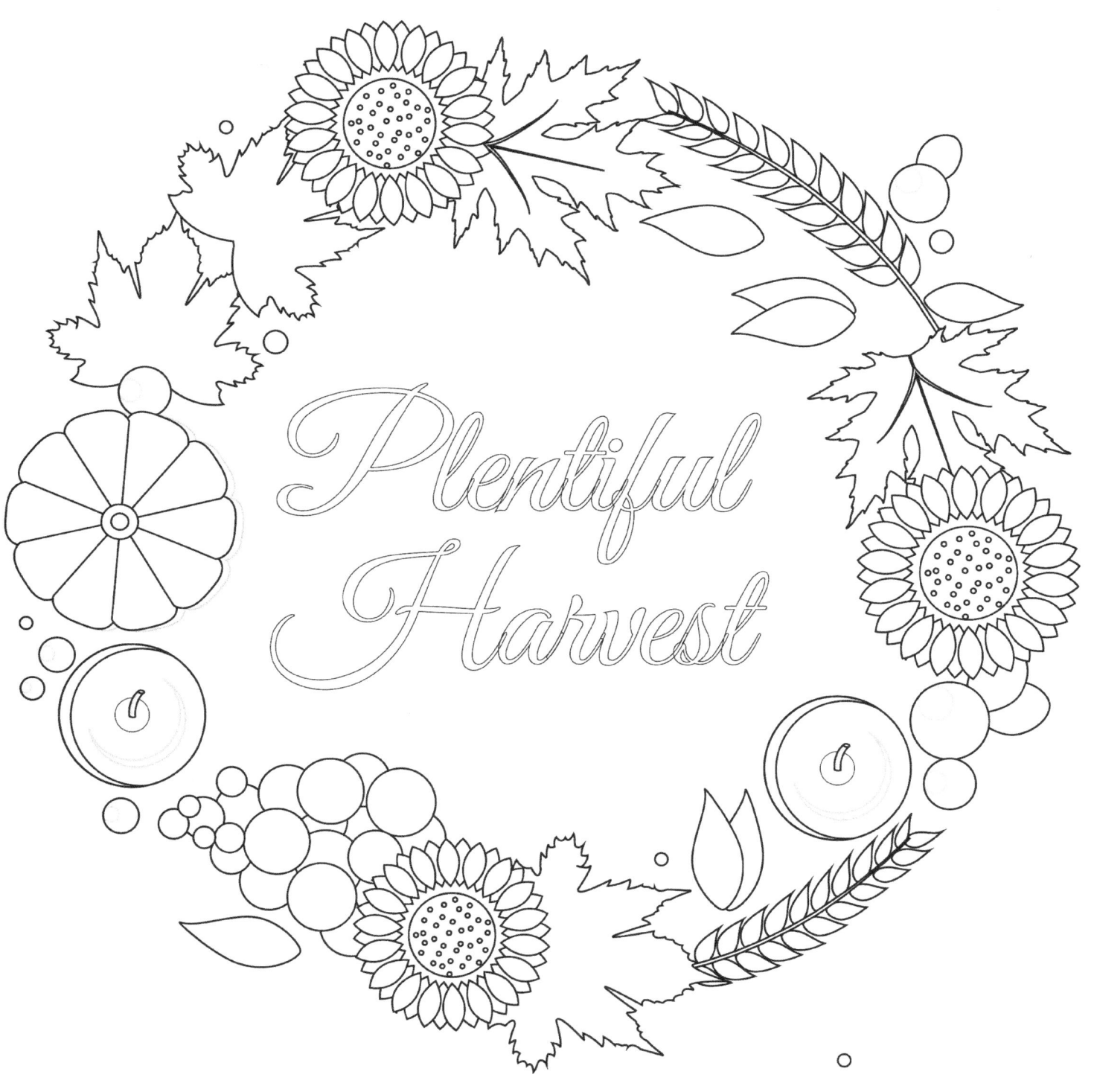

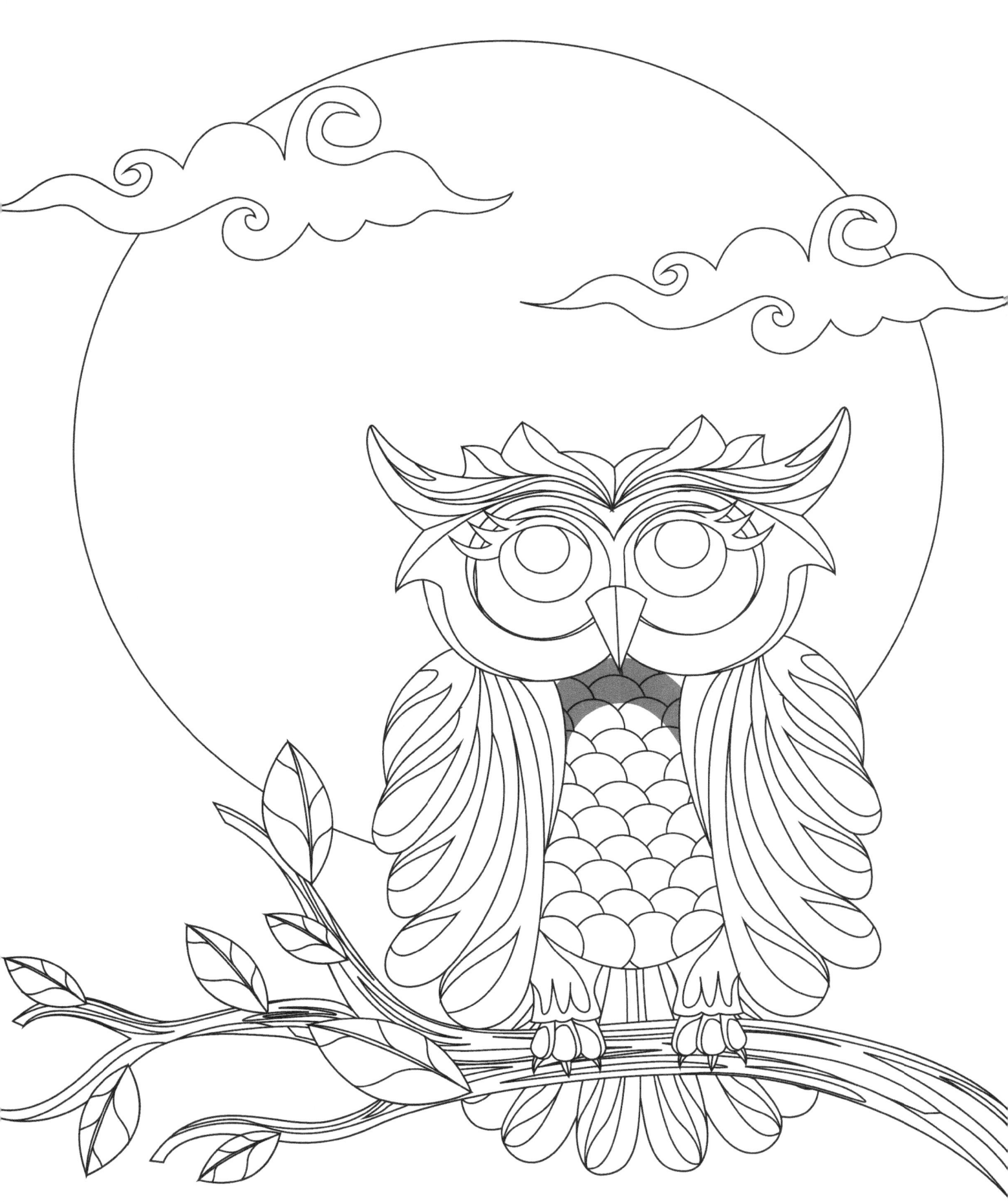

The End...

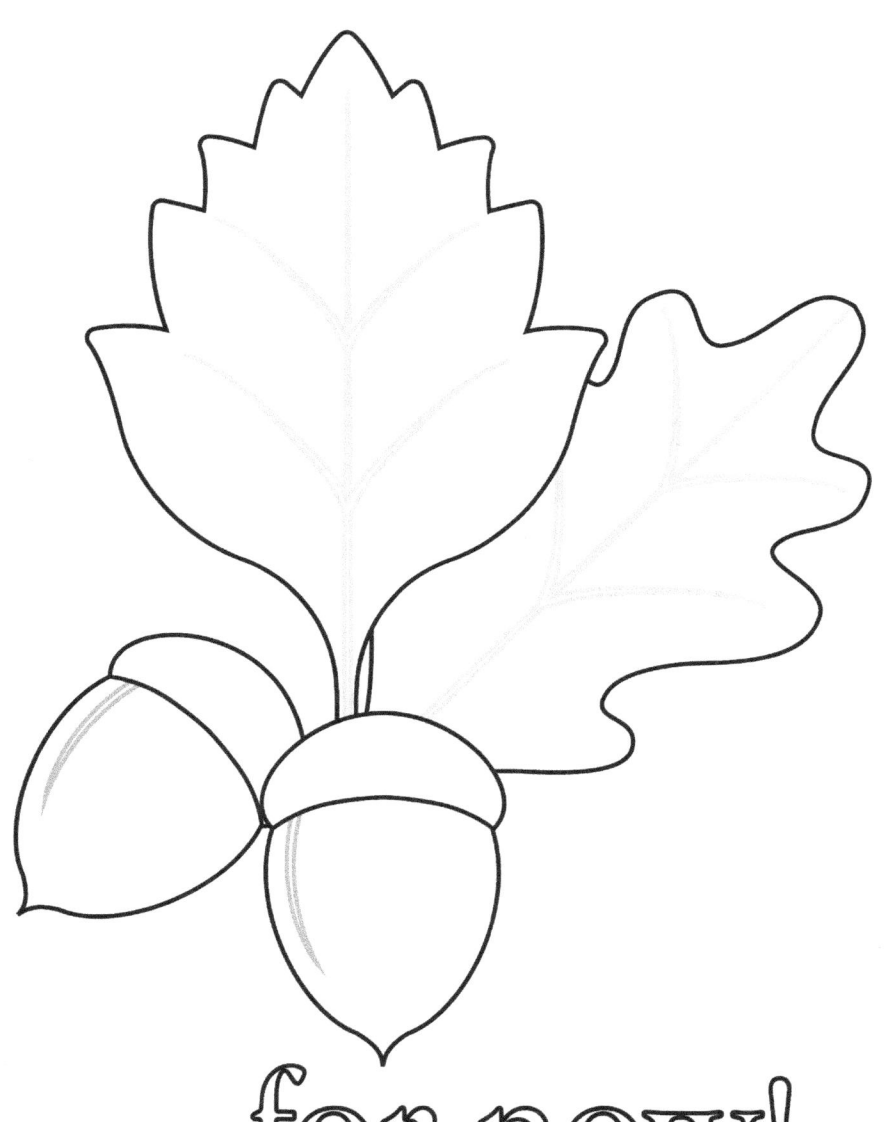

... for now!

HAVE YOU ENJOYED THIS *Oui Color* EXPERIENCE?

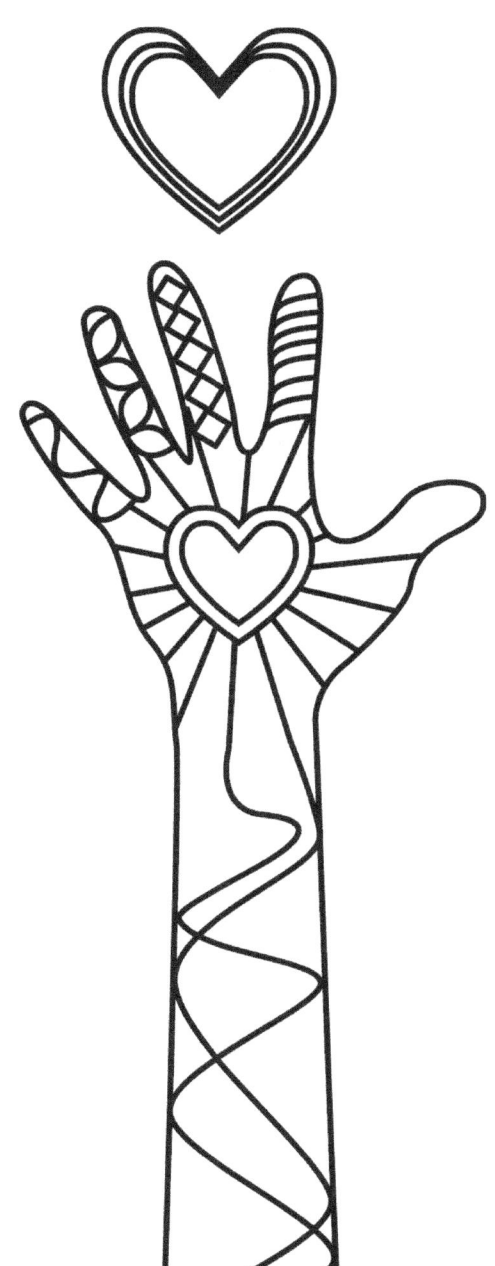

If so, I'd like to ask a teeny tiny favor that would make a WORLD of difference …

Would you take just a minute to leave an honest review?

It doesn't have to be long, just a sentence or two telling everyone what you liked about this coloring book. Your review and stars go a really long way toward letting others looking for coloring books know that they'll like this coloring book too!

Here's a direct link:

http://ouicolor.com/FallHarvest

Many, many Thank yous!

Color On!
-Sandra

OTHER BOOKS BY *Oui Color*:

Mandala Series
Centrè: 30 Designs to Get You Centered
Harmony: 30 Stress Reducing Designs
Zen: 30 Calming Mandala Designs

Pattern Series
Doodles: 30 Darling Patterns to Color, Vol. 1
Regal: 30 Royal Patterns to Color, Vol. 2
Milagros: 30 Magnificent Patterns to Color, Vol. 3

Nature Series
Oceans
Beautiful Butterflies & Fancy Flowers

FREE COLORING PAGES!
Visit www.ouicolor.com/FreeColoringPages
for more info.

NEW! Facebook Coloring Group - Join Us:
www.OuiColor.com/FacebookGroup

Follow *Oui Color* on
Twitter: @OuiColor
IG: OuiColor
Pinterest: www.pinterest.com/ouicolor

You can now upload your completed #OuiCreations
to the OuiGallery:
www.ouicolor.com/OuiGallery

#InspireYourCreativity

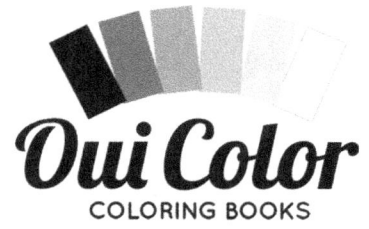

Oui Color
COLORING BOOKS

BLOTTER SHEET

Cut this sheet out with an Exacto blade
and use behind your chosen coloring page
to prevent bleed through!

Can also be used to test marker/pen/color pencil
colors before using on your work of art.

Oui Color
COLORING BOOKS

BLOTTER
SHEET

Cut this sheet out with an Exacto blade
and use behind your chosen coloring page
to prevent bleed through!

Can also be used to test marker/pen/color pencil
colors before using on your work of art.